DATE DUE

DATE DUE

GAYLORD   PRINTED IN U.S.A

GAYLORD M2G

RAP

SOUNDS OF MUSIC

David and Patricia Armentrout

The Rourke Corporation, Inc.
Vero Beach, Florida 32964

PHOTO CREDITS:
©Fotos International/Miranda Shen/Archive Photos: cover; ©Reuters/Steve Marcus/Archive Photos: title page; ©Bruce Carr: page 4; ©Oscar C. Williams: pages 7, 10, 21; ©Reuters/Evy Mages/Archive Photos: page 8; ©Fotos International/Archive Photos: page 12; ©Reuters/Fred Prouser/Archive Photos: page 13; ©Fotos International/Bob Scott/Archive Photos: page 15; ©Bill Stanton/Intl. Stock: pages 17, 18

PRODUCED BY:
East Coast Studios, Merritt Island, Florida

EDITORIAL SERVICES:
Susan Albury

Library of Congress Cataloging-in-Publication Data

Armentrout, David. 1962-
    Rap / by David and Patricia Armentrout.
      p. cm. — (Sounds of music)
    Includes bibliographical references (p. 24) and index.
    Summary: Discusses the origins, development and different aspects of the popular musical style, known as rap.
    ISBN 0-86593-531-9
    1. Rap (Music)—History and criticism Juvenile literature. [1. Rap (Music)]
I. Armentrout, Patricia, 1960- II. Title. III. Series
ML3531.A76 1999
782.421649—dc21   99-20058
                                                             CIP

TABLE OF CONTENTS

Express Yourself   5

Rap Music   6

The DJ   9

Rapping   11

Break Dancing   14

Scratching   16

Songs and Synthesizers   19

Music and Fashion   20

Rap Lyrics   22

Glossary   23

Index   24

Further Reading   24

EXPRESS YOURSELF

How do you express yourself? Talking is one way to express your feelings. Smiling, laughing, crying, and shouting are forms of expression, too.

Many people write stories, draw, and paint. Those activities are all forms of expression.

You can express yourself with music, too. As a matter of fact, people have been sharing their feelings through music and song for thousands of years.

Some people express themselves by the clothes they wear and the music they play.

RAP MUSIC

What is rap? Rap is a popular musical style. Rap is rhyming words spoken over music.

Rap is a form of self-expression. It can tell a story, teach a lesson, and prove a point. Rap **lyrics** (LEER iks) can send a powerful message.

Rap started with disc jockeys in the dance clubs of New York City. African Americans developed rap into a musical form in the 1970s, but rap didn't reach a big audience until the 1980s.

Fans surround the rapper's stage.

THE DJ

A disc jockey, or DJ, plays recorded music for others. A jamaican-born DJ named Kool DJ Herc showed off his deejaying style to **urban** (er BEN) black music lovers in New York City.

Kool DJ Herc had a unique style of repeating the musical breaks in a song. Herc did this by playing a record on one turntable and a copy on a second turntable.

Coke La Rock worked with Kool DJ Herc. La Rock "rapped" words and phrases during the musical breaks.

RAPPING

Rap lyrics are like poetry. Poetry verses, or lines, have a certain **rhythm** (RITH em).

In music, rhythm is the pattern of sound made by a combination of notes. In rap, rhythm is the pattern of sound you hear in the repeated rise and fall of the rapper's voice.

Rappers take advantage of rhythm and rhyme. Since rap is spoken, not sung, rappers use rhyming words and rhythm to create an interesting song.

Music lovers are entertained with rhythm and blues music and rap lyrics.

Kris Kross was the youngest successful rap duo.

Will Smith, also known as the Fresh Prince, performs with young dancers at his side.

BREAK DANCING

While DJs were having fun playing the musical breaks of a song, over and over, dancers felt compelled to show off their **acrobatic** (AK ruh BAT ik) talent.

These dancers were first nicknamed "b-boys," by Kool Herc. The b-boys kept the crowd excited and the party going. The b-boys performed dance movements that included splits and leg sweeps across the floor. The dancing became known as break dancing.

Kid-n-Play, known for their dance moves, have also made TV and movie appearances.

SCRATCHING

Scratching is a skill that early rap DJs used to produce a musical sound. The sound did not come from a familiar, or normal, musical instrument. It came from a record turntable.

To produce the "scratchy" **percussion** (per KUSH en) sound, the DJ moved a record back and forth allowing the turntable needle to scratch the record's surface. Some DJs also played a musical break from a song at the same time.

A new musical sound was made by scratching a record's surface.

SONGS AND SYNTHESIZERS

At first, artists rapped to bits and pieces of older songs, or to electronic music from **synthesizers** (SIN thuh size erz) and drum machines.

Some rappers still choose to rap to electronic music. Other rappers perform with a band. The members play rhythm and blues or even hard rock-style music.

Some rappers recycle old songs by rapping part or all of the lyrics. The finished product sounds a bit familiar but with that new **hip-hop** (hip hop) style.

Rappers use synthesizers to create different musical sounds.

19

MUSIC AND FASHION

Many performers pay close attention to what fashion designers are making. Performers like to wear what is new and different.

Fashion is a form of self-expression just like music. Rap artists sparked a new fashion— especially with teenagers. Many rappers wear baseball caps, long baggy pants, and other loose-fitting clothes. Fans copied the rap, or hip-hop, style which helped to spread a new fashion trend.

The baggy clothing style was inspired by the hip-hop culture.

RAP LYRICS

Rap artists rap about personal experience. Some tell of politics, religion, love, and even death. Some rap music has gotten a "bad rap." That's because the lyrics include bad language, and tell about the worst parts of society—like drug use and violence.

Many rappers understand that their music can sway young people. These rappers select their lyrics carefully. They choose not to be a bad influence, but to simply entertain their fans with their sounds of music.

GLOSSARY

acrobatic (AK ruh BAT ik) — gymnastic-like movement

hip-hop (hip hop) — a term that started as a rap rhyme but now defines rap music, break dancing, graffiti, and performers and followers of the rap culture

lyrics (LEER iks) — the words of a song

percussion (per KUSH en) — instruments where the sound comes from striking, beating, or scraping

rhythm (RITH em) — a combination of notes with long and short sounds and rests

synthesizer (SIN thuh size er) — a system of generators that make and control sound

urban (er BEN) — relating to the city

INDEX

b-boys   14
break dancing   14
Coke La Rock   9
disc jockey   6, 9, 14, 16
electronic music   19
hip-hop   19, 20, 21
Kool DJ Herc   9, 14
Kris Kross   12
LL Cool J   8

lyrics   6, 22
Queen Latifah   8
rhyme   6, 11
rhythm   11
rhythm and blues   19
rock   19
scratching   16, 17
Smith, Will   13
synthesizers   18, 19
turntable   9, 16

FURTHER READING

Find out more about music with these helpful books and information sources:

• Rose, Tricia. *Black Noise: Rap Music and Black Culture in Contemporary America.* Music/Culture Series. Wesleyan University Press, 1994
• Sexton, Adam. *Rap on Rap: Straight-up Talk on Hip Hop Culture.* Dell Publishing, 1995
• Stancell, Steven. *Rap Whoz Who: The World of Rap Music.* Schirmer Books, 1996
• "Rap Music." Grolier Multimedia Encyclopedia, 1998
• "Rap." Microsoft Encarta Encyclopedia, 1996